Childhoods
of the
Presidents

Theodore Roosevelt

Childhoods *of the* Presidents

John Adams

George W. Bush

Bill Clinton

Ulysses S. Grant

Andrew Jackson

Thomas Jefferson

John F. Kennedy

Abraham Lincoln

James Madison

James Monroe

Ronald Reagan

Franklin D. Roosevelt

Theodore Roosevelt

Harry S. Truman

George Washington

Woodrow Wilson

Theodore Roosevelt

Hal Marcovitz

Mason Crest Publishers
Philadelphia

Produced by OTTN Publishing, Stockton, New Jersey

Mason Crest Publishers
370 Reed Road
Broomall, PA 19008
www.masoncrest.com

First printing

1 3 5 7 9 8 6 4 2

Library of Congress Cataloging-in-Publication Data

Marcovitz, Hal.
   Theodore Roosevelt / Hal Marcovitz.
     p. cm.   (Childhood of the presidents)
   Summary: A biography of the twenty-sixth president of the United States, focusing on his childhood and young adulthood.
   Includes bibliographical references and index.
    ISBN 1-59084-278-2 (hc.)
   1. Roosevelt, Theodore, 1858-1919—Juvenile literature.
   2. Roosevelt, Theodore, 1858-1919—Childhood and youth—Juvenile literature. 3. Presidents—United States—Biography—Juvenile literature. [1. Roosevelt, Theodore, 1858-1919—Childhood and youth. 2. Presidents.] I. Title. II. Series.
E757.M36 2003
973.91'1'092—dc21
[B]   2002024437

Publisher's note: All quotations in this book come from original sources, and contain the spelling and grammatical inconsistencies of the original text.

Childhoods
of the
Presidents

Table of Contents

★★★★★★★★★★★★★★★★★★

★ *Introduction* ★

Alexis de Tocqueville began his great work *Democracy in America* with a discourse on childhood. If we are to understand the prejudices, the habits and the passions that will rule a man's life, Tocqueville said, we must watch the baby in his mother's arms; we must see the first images that the world casts upon the mirror of his mind; we must hear the first words that awaken his sleeping powers of thought. "The entire man," he wrote, "is, so to speak, to be seen in the cradle of the child."

That is why these books on the childhoods of the American presidents are so much to the point. And, as our history shows, a great variety of childhoods can lead to the White House. The record confirms the ancient adage that every American boy, no matter how unpromising his beginnings, can aspire to the presidency. Soon, one hopes, the adage will be extended to include every American girl.

All our presidents thus far have been white males who, within the limits of their gender, reflect the diversity of American life. They were born in nineteen of our states; eight of the last thirteen presidents were born west of the Mississippi. Of all our presidents, Abraham Lincoln had the least promising childhood, yet he became our greatest president. Oddly enough, presidents who are children of privilege sometimes feel an obligation to reform society in order to give children of poverty a better break. And, with Lincoln the great exception, presidents who are children of poverty sometimes feel that there is no need to reform a society that has enabled them to rise from privation to the summit.

Does schooling make a difference? Harry S. Truman, the only twentieth-century president never to attend college, is generally accounted a near-great president. Actually nine—more than one fifth—of our presidents never went to college at all, including such luminaries as George Washington, Andrew Jackson and Grover Cleveland. But, Truman aside, all the non-college men held the highest office before the twentieth century, and, given the increasing complexity of life, a college education will unquestionably be a necessity in the twenty-first century.

Every reader of this book, girls included, has a right to aspire to the presidency. As you survey the childhoods of those who made it, try to figure out the qualities that brought them to the White House. I would suggest that among those qualities are ambition, determination, discipline, education—and luck.

—ARTHUR M. SCHLESINGER, JR.

Theodore Roosevelt was a boxer and wrestler at Harvard when this photo was taken, around 1875. Physically, he'd come a long way from the skinny, sickly boy who just three years earlier had been roughed up in a stagecoach.

A Born Fighter

![wavy lines decoration]

Fourteen-year-old Theodore Roosevelt sat in the stage-coach as it bounced along the dusty, unpaved roads of New England in 1872. He was a thin and *sickly* boy who wore thick glasses and suffered terribly from asthma, a medical disorder caused by allergies that makes it difficult to breathe. Still, young Theodore—who was called "Teedie" by his parents—had a zest for life and refused to allow his asthma to get in the way of his many interests. Teedie had a fascination with science, and he was particularly interested in birds and other wildlife. When he grew older, he planned to pursue a career in science.

Still, there were times when "the asmer," as he called it, became almost unbearable, causing him to cough and wheeze uncontrollably. His parents, Martha and Theodore Roosevelt Sr., were convinced the asthma was caused by the stuffy, polluted air that hung over the family's home in New York City. Whenever Teedie's asthma seemed particularly bad, his mother and father would make arrangements to take the boy into the country.

The Roosevelts were a wealthy family and could afford the

luxuries of splendid countryside vacation homes. This year, with Teedie's asthma troubling him severely, his parents had decided once again to send him out of the city. Teedie was now old enough to travel alone, so the Roosevelts had booked passage for him on the stagecoach. It was heading for Moosehead Lake in Maine, where the boy would stay in a cabin until his asthma improved.

On the trip north, Teedie found himself sharing the stage-coach with two older boys. Bored from the long trip aboard the tiny and uncomfortable stagecoach, the two boys decided to make sport of the skinny kid with the glasses. Teedie was no meek little lamb—he had always had the courage to stand up for himself—but in this case he was overmatched.

"I have no doubt they were good-hearted boys, but they were boys!" Teddy Roosevelt, as he would become known later in life, recalled. "They found that I was a foreordained and predestined victim, and industriously proceeded to make life miserable for me. The worst feature was that when I finally tried to fight them I discovered that either one singly could not only handle me with easy contempt, but handle me so as not to hurt me much and yet prevent my doing any damage whatever in return."

Teedie did not intend to go through life being bullied by older boys. When he returned to New York, he informed his father that he intended to take boxing lessons so that he could defend himself. Theodore Roosevelt Sr. was delighted with his son's decision. He was a strong advocate of physical fitness and believed that Teedie's problems with asthma could be solved if he developed his body.

Moosehead Lake in Maine (shown here) was Teedie Roosevelt's destination during his fateful stagecoach ride of 1872.

"Theodore, you have the mind, but you have not the body, and without the help of the body the mind cannot go as far as it should," Theodore Sr. told his son. "You must make your body. It is hard drudgery to make one's body, but I know you will do it." Teedie clenched his teeth. "I'll make my body," he declared.

Teedie's father searched the gyms of New York for a suitable boxing instructor. He finally hired John Long to tutor his son in the techniques of self-defense. Long had been a *prizefighter* himself, and he was now a trainer of some of New

York's most famous professional boxers. This was before there were many rules in boxing and even before organizations were established to regulate the sport. When Theodore Roosevelt learned how to box, professionals fought with "bare knuckles," meaning they didn't wear the heavy, padded boxing gloves that today's fighters wear.

Teedie was an enthusiastic student. For months, he trained at Long's gym. When he wasn't working with his teacher in the ring, he concentrated on developing his muscles. He performed exercises and lifted weights to increase his strength and endurance.

Theodore Sr. bought some exercise equipment and had it installed in the family's backyard garden in New York so that Teedie could also train at home. Family members could often find the young fitness enthusiast in the garden exercising among the azaleas and tiger lilies while the Roosevelts' pet peacocks strutted nearby.

Teedie's sister Corinne later said, "For many years one of my most vivid recollections is seeing him between the horizontal bars, widening his chest by regular, monotonous motion—drudgery indeed."

All that work paid off. While in training, Teedie was much less troubled by asthma.

Theodore Roosevelt enjoyed other sports besides boxing. As president, he helped write new rules for football designed to end unnecessary violence in the game. He also helped form the National Collegiate Athletic Association.

One day, Long held a competition among his students. They would box each other, and the winners would be awarded cheap drinking mugs made of pewter, a rough, dull metal often used to fashion utensils for the dinner table. Teedie was still one of the smaller students training at the gym. Long entered him in the competition among boys in the lightweight class.

"Neither he nor I had any idea that I could do anything, but I was entered in the lightweight contest, in which it happened that I was pitted in succession against a couple of reedy striplings who were even worse than I was," Teddy Roosevelt later wrote. "Equally to their surprise and to my own, and to John Long's, I won, and the pewter mug became one of my most prized possessions. I kept it . . . and fear I bragged about it, for a number of years."

As he grew older, Theodore Roosevelt would remain an enthusiast of the sport of boxing. While attending Harvard University, he joined the boxing and wrestling teams and took up jujitsu, a Japanese martial art. Later, as police commissioner of New York City, he could often be found at ringside cheering on a favorite boxer.

And in 1901, when Theodore Roosevelt became president of the United States, he continued to enjoy the sport of boxing. In fact, he would often take a break from his duties in the White House to spar with professional boxers. One of those boxers was Mike Donovan.

"Had he come to the prize ring, instead of the political arena, it is my conviction that he would have been successful," Donovan said. "He is a born fighter."

A House Divided

The first Roosevelts arrived in America in 1649. They were Dutch settlers who established farms in the colony of New Amsterdam. By the time the colony became known as New York, the Roosevelts were successful farmers, merchants, bankers, manufacturers, and engineers. The family soon became part of the fabric of America. One of the Roosevelt family's *ancestors* traveled across the Atlantic with William Penn, founder of Pennsylvania. Roosevelts served in the Continental Congress and fought in the Revolutionary War.

By the time Theodore Roosevelt Sr. was 27 years old, he was already wealthy in his own right. He was the owner of Roosevelt and Son, a family-owned import company, which bought goods from factories in Europe and sold them to stores in America. Theodore Sr. also married into a wealthy family. Martha Bulloch Roosevelt, whom everybody in the family called Mittie, was the daughter of a Georgia plantation owner.

"He combined strength and courage with gentleness, tenderness, and great unselfishness," Theodore Roosevelt would say about his father, who is depicted in this portrait. "He would not tolerate in us children selfishness or cruelty, idleness, cowardice or untruthfulness."

The Roosevelts were a happy and close family, but there was no question that dark days were ahead for them as well as for everyone else in America. By the 1850s, it was clear that America was heading for civil war. Indeed, the Roosevelts would be a house divided. Theodore Roosevelt Sr. was a patriotic American and member of the Republican Party, the new political organization that would soon nominate Abraham Lincoln for the presidency. Mittie Roosevelt was a daughter of the South. Her family owned slaves, and her brothers would eventually join the Confederacy's navy.

Still, thoughts of war were far from the minds of Theodore and Mittie Roosevelt on the afternoon of October 27, 1858. Theodore Jr. was born that day in the Roosevelt home at 28 East 20th Street in New York. He was the second child of Theodore and Mittie. A daughter, Anna, who was called "Bamie," had been born six years earlier. After Teedie, the Roosevelts would have two more children: Elliott, nearly two years younger than Teedie, and Corinne, a year younger than Elliott.

Two other people lived in the Roosevelt home. They were Martha Bulloch, Mittie's mother, whom the children called "Grandmamma," and Mittie's sister Annie, who taught the four Roosevelt children.

Teedie adored his father the most. "My father, Theodore Roosevelt, was the best man I ever knew," he later wrote. "He combined strength and courage with gentleness, tenderness, and great unselfishness."

Unknown to Teedie, though, his father was facing a great personal decision that troubled him deeply. On April 12, 1861, Southern cannons opened fire on Fort Sumter in South

Carolina, touching off the Civil War. As a man of youth and good health, Theodore Roosevelt Sr. would be expected to accept a commission in the Union army. But Teedie's father was concerned about his family and business obligations. He was also worried about the effect his service on the battlefield would have on his marriage. Mittie had already made it known to her husband that she sympathized with the Southern cause. Once she even flew the Confederate flag in front of the house on East 20th Street. What if he were forced to face Mittie's two brothers in battle? How could he fire on family?

"I wish we sympathized together on this question of so vital moment to our country," he told Mittie. "I know you cannot understand my feelings and of course do not expect it."

Teedie's father spent months agonizing over what to do. Finally, he decided that he would not serve in the Union army. Although Congress had approved a draft, in which young men are called up to serve in the army, the lawmakers had included a provision for draftees to hire substitutes to serve in their places. Theodore Roosevelt Sr. hired a substitute, as did other wealthy Northerners. It was a practice that prompted many soldiers to complain, "rich man's war, poor man's fight."

As he grew older the future president spoke little about his father's decision to stay out of the line of fire. However, Theodore himself was very active in the military. During the Spanish-American War in 1898, Theodore joined a crack company of cavalry soldiers known as the Rough Riders. Theodore was second-in-command of the unit and led the Rough Riders in a famous charge up San Juan Hill in Cuba. During World War I, Theodore Roosevelt encouraged his four sons to join the American Expeditionary Force, the army that fought in France. His youngest son, Quentin, was killed in battle.

Although Theodore Sr. chose not to carry a weapon, he still intended to support the war effort. In the early days of the war, it became clear to government officials that many of the Union soldiers were being enticed to spend their pay by liquor salesmen and other *devious* merchants who visited the camps and charged high prices for their goods. Many soldiers were also losing their pay in the never-ending gambling games that were a part of every camp. To address the problem, Theodore Roosevelt Sr. convinced Congress to create an "Allotment Commission." The commission was charged with enrolling soldiers in a program that would send most of their pay directly home to their families. Teedie's father was appointed one of three allotment commissioners.

This meant that for the duration of the Civil War, Theodore Sr. would be mostly on the road, visiting army camps and talking to the soldiers about the allotment program. Young Teedie was only two years old when his father left for his war service. He hardly missed him at first, but as the war dragged on and the boy grew older, he began to realize that his beloved father was no longer a part of his life.

"Teedie is the most affectionate and endearing little creature in his ways but begins to require Papa's discipline rather sadly," wrote his mother. "He is brimming full of mischief and has to be watched all the time."

The Civil War years were difficult for Teedie to bear in other ways. It was during this time that the boy's asthma developed. The other children suffered ailments as well. Bamie had a defect in her spine, Elliott was prone to colds and fever, and Corinne would soon develop asthma, too.

The Roosevelt family, 1872 or early 1873. The four children are sitting on the floor in the front. From left: Anna, Corinne, Teedie, Elliott. Theodore Roosevelt Sr. is seated at the center; to his right is his wife, Mittie.

Occasionally, Theodore Sr. would return home from his duty in the army camps and find his once-happy family beset by illness. What's more, the war was not going well for the South, a circumstance that forced Mittie into a deep depression. Her two brothers had fled to England during the war. Bamie recalled that Mittie would lock herself in a bedroom whenever her husband's friends came to the house. One of Theodore Sr.'s best friends was John Hay, President Abraham Lincoln's personal secretary, and he visited the Roosevelt home often. Others who dropped by the house on East 20th Street from time to time were the Union generals Ulysses S. Grant, William Tecumseh Sherman, and George McClellan. Their talk usually turned to news of the war, and Mittie couldn't bear to listen.

The funeral procession of Abraham Lincoln nears Union Square in New York City, 1865. The two figures at the second-floor side window of the white house with shutters are thought to be Teedie and Elliott Roosevelt.

"She must have been homesick for her own people until her heart bled in those early days," Bamie later said.

Near the end of the war, troops under General Sherman looted Mittie's home in Georgia when they swept through the

South on their "March to the Sea." Years later, after Theodore became president, a former soldier in Sherman's army sent him a book of poetry that he had stolen from Mittie's house.

Unknown to her husband, Mittie was helping the Southern cause. When Theodore Sr. left home to return to his Allotment Commission duties, Mittie, along with her mother and sister, packed food, clothes, and medical supplies into boxes, which they shipped to the Confederate army. Little Teedie was often drafted to help with the labors. One time, he recalled, he became angry with his mother and decided to hurt her by pledging his allegiance to the Union. "I attempted a partial vengeance by praying with loud fervor for the success of Union arms when we all came to say our prayers before my mother in the evening," he said. During his prayers, he asked God to "grind the Southern troops to powder."

Instead of becoming upset with her son, Mittie laughed.

Finally, the war ended. The victorious Union troops returned home, often in grand parades while thousands of people cheered.

Not all of those parades featured cheering, however. Five days after the South surrendered, a Confederate sympathizer named John Wilkes Booth shot Abraham Lincoln. The body of the dead president was carried in a slow funeral procession across the country. On April 25, 1865, the parade made its way past Union Square in New York City and the home of Cornelius Roosevelt, Teedie's grandfather. Teedie and Elliott stood at the second-floor window of their grandfather's home that day, gazing down on the sad procession that carried the body of the president.

One of Theodore Roosevelt's childhood pictures. From an early age he was keenly interested in nature. As president he would remain a devoted conservationist, setting aside millions of acres of public land for wildlife sanctuaries, national forests, and national parks—a priceless gift to future generations.

The Young Naturalist

*T*eedie was fascinated by the books he found in his father's library at the home on East 20th Street. One of his favorite books was *Missionary Travels and Researches in Southern Africa*. It was a huge book containing dozens of pictures of African wildlife. In the book, he saw pictures of herds of zebra grazing in the tall grass, hippopotamuses sunning themselves in murky rivers, elephants ambling through dense rain forests, and dozens of other animals. The book even featured insects of what was then called the "Dark Continent." Teedie found a picture of a tsetse fly as big as his hand and was immediately enthralled.

For Teedie, it would be the beginning of a lifelong love for nature. As an adult, he would become an avid outdoorsman, hiking, camping, hunting, and riding horseback through the rugged countryside of America. As president, his efforts as a *conservationist* would result in the creation of a system of national parks and forests that preserved some 230 million acres of American land.

His father owned other books about wildlife and nature. Teedie spent hours sitting in a stuffed red velvet chair in the

library, paging through the books and devouring the informa-
tion they had to offer. The red velvet chair became such a part
of his life that his mother had his birthday pictures taken in it.

Soon he was drawing his own pictures of wildlife. He
always included descriptions of the creatures as well as his
observations of their habits. Mostly, the bugs and animals on
the list were limited to what he could find in the backyard garden of the Roosevelt home: ants, spiders, beetles, dragonflies,
mice, and birds. He was particularly interested in the birds. By
the time he was 10 years old, Teedie had resolved to pursue a
career as a *zoologist*. He vividly recalled the incident that had
convinced him his life would be spent studying animals:

> I was walking up Broadway, and as I passed the market to which I used
> sometimes to be sent before breakfast to get strawberries I suddenly saw
> a dead seal laid out on a slab of wood. That seal filled me with every pos-
> sible feeling of romance and adventure. I asked where it was killed, and
> [was] informed in the harbor. . . . As long as that seal remained there I
> haunted the neighborhood of the market day after day. I measured it,
> and I recall that, not having a tape measure, I had to do my best to get its
> *girth* with a folding pocket foot-rule, a difficult undertaking. I carefully
> made a record of the utterly useless measurements, and at once began to
> write a natural history of my own, on the strength of that seal.

Teedie combed the garden behind the home as well as the
many parks of New York City in search of tiny animals, birds,
bugs, and spiders that he could draw, describe, collect, and
even *dissect*. His room at 28 East 20th Street took on the look
of a museum and, in fact, Teedie named the collection the
"Roosevelt Museum of Natural History." Soon, the collection
started spilling over into the rest of the house.

Teedie closed a letter to his sister Anna with this tongue-in-cheek illustration of Darwin's theory of evolution at work. He depicted himself as having evolved from a stork; his brother, Elliott, from a bull; and his cousin John Elliott, from a monkey.

Guests reaching for the water pitcher in the parlor were occasionally surprised by snakes swimming lazily in the warm drinking water. The domestic staff found all manner of little critters under their feet and threatened to quit. "How can I do the laundry with a snapping turtle tied to the legs of the sink?" complained the washerwoman. The cook said, "Either I leave or the woodchuck does." When his mother found a box of dead mice in the icebox and threw them out in disgust, Teedie cried, "The loss to science, the loss to science!"

Despite his tangles with family members and the household staff over his collection, Teedie regarded his work as a serious study of wildlife and wrote extensive notes on what he observed. A tree spider, he wrote, "is grey-spotted and black" and lives "in communities of about 20" under patches of loose bark. He said the spider's web "looks exactly like some cotton on the top but if you take that off you will see several small webs . . . each having several little occupants."

Teedie decided to collect his observations into books, which he wrote out in longhand. His first book was titled "The Broadway Seal." It included his observations and scientific analysis of the seal he had seen dead on the New York docks. He was aided in his work by the kindness of the local butcher, who gave him the seal's skull.

His next project was "The Foregoing Ant," which explained why ants always seem to walk forward. Next, he moved up to a more comprehensive work on insect life, which he titled "Natural History of Insects."

"All the insects I write about in this book inhabit North America. Now and then a friend has told me something about them but mostly I have gained their habits from observation," Teedie wrote in the book's introduction.

In the book, Teedie detailed what he observed about beetles, dragonflies, ants, spiders, ladybugs, and lightning bugs, but he also mentioned various birds and aquatic animals. Sometimes, his powers of observation didn't appear to be up to the task at hand. Describing the lobster, for example, Teedie found it, well, indescribable. "Look at the lobster and you have its form," he explained to his readers.

Teedie's interest in nature was not limited to the little bugs and animals he found underfoot. As a young boy he discovered the books of Mayne Reid, an author who wrote about trappers, traders, cowboys, and other frontiersmen exploring lands of adventure and mystery filled with wildlife Teedie would never find in the backyard. Teedie spent hours at home, curled up in the red velvet library chair, devouring Reid's books and dreaming of the life of an adventurer.

"I experienced a buoyancy of spirits and vigor of body I had never known before," he wrote later. "I felt a pleasure in action. My blood seemed to rush warmer and swifter through my veins, and I fancied my eyes reached to a more distant vision."

In fact, Teedie soon discovered a real fact about his "distant vision." It wasn't very good. For his 13th birthday, his father gave him a shotgun, which he happily toted to some nearby woods. There he discovered that his aim was dreadful. At first he thought the gun was defective, but his friends tried it out and had no trouble hitting their marks. He reported this incident to his father, who correctly deduced the problem: the boy was *nearsighted*. Teedie was fitted with glasses.

"I had no idea how beautiful the world was until I got those spectacles," he wrote. "I had been a clumsy and awkward little boy, and while much of my clumsiness and awkwardness was doubtless due to general characteristics, a good deal of it was due to the fact that I could not see and yet was wholly ignorant that I was not seeing."

The spectacles had arrived just in time, for in a short while young Theodore Roosevelt would learn that there was much more to see in the world than he had imagined.

Teedie (left), Elliott, and Corrine Roosevelt, along with their cousins Maud (center) and John Elliott (right), look bored in this 1873 portrait, taken during an overseas trip. But the trip itself—to Egypt, the Middle East, and Europe—proved anything but boring.

A Thousand Thoughts

*T*he riders moved slowly along the plains just outside Damascus, Syria. One of the riders was Teedie; the other, an Arab guide named Bootross. Suddenly, a pair of *jackals* streaked across their paths. Teedie kicked his horse to a gallop and shouted for Bootross to follow. The jackals led the pair on an exciting chase. For Teedie, it was an adventure right out of a Mayne Reid story.

"Bootross was on bad ground and could not get near the beasts," Teedie wrote. "[The jackals] separated and I went after the largest. . . . On we went over hills, and through gulleys, where none but a Syrian horse could go. I gained rapidly on him and was within a few yards of him when he leaped over a cliff some fifteen feet high, and while I made a detour around he got in among some rocky hills where I could not get him."

The jackal got away, but otherwise the Roosevelt family's trip to North Africa and the Middle East had been an excellent experience for Teedie. The journey introduced him to customs and societies that he had only read about, as well as many forms of plant and animal life that he could never see in the parks near East 20th Street in New York.

Teedie's overseas adventure began in the fall of 1872, when Theodore Roosevelt Sr. decided to take his family on a tour of Egypt and the Middle East, followed by visits to several European countries. Three years before, the Roosevelts had made their first visit to Europe, but the children had hardly enjoyed themselves. Much of the time illness had dogged the three youngest children, particularly Teedie, who suffered several serious asthma attacks. But now, with the children older, Theodore Sr. and Mittie decided Teedie, Bamie, Elliott, and Corinne could learn much from another trip overseas.

In October, the Roosevelts had boarded a ship in New York Harbor and sailed to Liverpool in England. After crossing the English Channel by boat, the Roosevelts traveled overland through Europe. They then boarded another boat that sailed across the Mediterranean Sea, finally landing in port in Cairo, Egypt, on November 28.

"It was a sight to awaken a thousand thoughts," Teedie Roosevelt wrote in his diary about Egypt. Here, a boat sails up the Nile River, a journey that the Roosevelt family also made and that Teedie greatly enjoyed. On the opposite page are the Sphinx and Great Pyramid at Giza, which the Roosevelts visited while in Egypt.

"How I gazed upon it!" Teedie wrote in his diary. "It was Egypt, the land of my dreams; Egypt, the most ancient of all countries. . . . It was a sight to awaken a thousand thoughts, and it did." In Egypt, the family toured *mosques*, as well as the Great Pyramid, the open markets of Cairo, and the deserts and bogs that surround the city. Finally, the family boarded a houseboat known as a *dahabeah* and set off for a slow voyage south on the Nile River.

Sailing up the river, Teedie saw tropical birds circling overhead, camels ambling slowly along, water buffalo standing lazily in the river, and zebus sunning themselves along the banks. Zebus are large animals with humps and horns that resemble oxen.

There were plenty of opportunities for Teedie and the other children to go ashore and explore. The *dahabeah* made many stops, and Teedie, Elliott, and Corinne hopped off the boat to wade among the reeds in the murky Nile waters. Teedie used the stopovers to collect birds. For Christmas, his father had given him a new shotgun. Now, with his vision corrected, his aim had improved. Teedie took the birds he shot back to the deck of the *dahabeah*, where he dissected them with instruments he had brought from home.

"The bird collecting gave what was really the chief zest

> The Roosevelt family was well represented in the White House in the first half of the 20th century. Theodore Roosevelt's niece Eleanor married her distant cousin, Franklin Delano Roosevelt, who would follow Theodore into the White House. While president, Theodore Roosevelt gave away the bride at the wedding of Franklin and Eleanor.

of my Nile journey," he wrote. "I was old enough and had read enough to enjoy the temples and the desert scenery and the general feeling of romance; but this in time would have palled if I had not also had the serious work of collecting and preparing my specimens."

In late January they left the *dahabeah* and headed north to visit Syria, Turkey, and Palestine. In Palestine, most of which is now part of the country of Israel, the children went swimming in the Jordan River. In Turkey, they toured the ancient city of Constantinople, which is now known as Istanbul.

From Turkey, the family toured Greece and Austria before making their way to Germany, where Theodore Sr. had already decided that Teedie, Elliott, and Corinne should remain for several months to study. In the city of Dresden, the Minkwitz family agreed to provide a home for the children as well as teach them the German language. One of the Minkwitz sons was an accomplished swordsman, and Teedie was delighted when the boy agreed to give him fencing lessons.

Teedie, Elliott, and Corinne plunged into their studies, learning not only German but also mathematics from the Minkwitzes. As for Teedie, he continued his scientific pursuits, collecting and dissecting animals he found in the near-

> Theodore Roosevelt never lost his love of adventure. He was the first former president to fly in an airplane. The flight occurred in 1910 and lasted just a few seconds. After landing, Roosevelt said, "This is bully!"

by woods. *Frau* Minkwitz refused to tolerate the odors of the mammal and reptile skins that Teedie brought into the house, and she made him hang them outside. One night, during a

A 19th-century painting of Dresden, the beautiful German city where Teedie Roosevelt and his younger brother and sister lived and studied for several months in 1873.

terrible storm that had everyone in the house hiding beneath their covers, Teedie suddenly said, "Oh, it is raining and my hedgehog will be all spoiled."

The Minkwitzes were impressed with the Roosevelt children, particularly Teedie. He seemed to be the hardest-working and most **bookish** of the three children. And even though he still suffered from attacks of asthma, he never neglected his studies. He had a thirst for knowledge that was never quenched.

Teedie's days in Dresden were never idle. Here is how he described a typical day in the Minkwitz home: "Halfpast six, up and breakfast which is through at halfpast seven, when we study till nine; repeat till halfpast twelve, have lunch, and study till three, when we take coffee and have free time till tea, at seven. After tea we study till ten, when we go to bed. It is harder than I ever studied in my life, but I like it for I really feel that I am making considerable progress."

After dropping the children off in Dresden, Theodore Sr., Mittie, and Bamie continued to travel in Europe. Occasionally, Mittie would return to Dresden to check on the well-being of her children. As Mittie prepared to leave the Minkwitz home after a short visit, she told Frau Minkwitz that she was particularly concerned about Teedie, her sickly son.

Frau Minkwitz replied, "You need not be anxious about him. He will surely one day be a great professor, or who knows, he may become even president of the United States."

The Story of the Teddy Bear

While hunting, President Theodore Roosevelt refused to shoot an old, injured bear. His guides named the bear "Teddy" after the president. Over time, the story changed with the telling and the bear became a cute and cuddly cub. The incident inspired the popular stuffed toys called teddy bears.

A portrait of Theodore Roosevelt, who became the nation's 26th president following the assassination of William McKinley in 1901.

The Bull Moose

*L*eon Czolgosz was an immigrant from Poland who found little but poverty and misery in America. By 1901, he had left his job in a wire factory to become an anarchist, a person who opposes organized authority and believes in the use of violence to improve the lives of the working class.

Czolgosz read in the newspaper that President William F. McKinley planned to travel to Buffalo, New York, to attend the Pan American Exposition, an event similar to a World's Fair. Czolgosz decided to kill the president. He bought a gun, left his home in Cleveland, Ohio, and headed for Buffalo.

He carried out his plans on September 6. Czolgosz waited at the Temple of Music to shake the president's hand. When McKinley extended his hand to Czolgosz, the anarchist drew his gun and fired. McKinley died in a hospital eight days later.

Under the terms of the U.S. Constitution, if the president dies in office, the vice president ascends to the presidency. McKinley's vice president was Theodore Roosevelt. He took the oath of office on September 14, 1901.

Roosevelt's entry into the White House capped a career in public service that began shortly after he graduated from

Theodore Roosevelt leads the Rough Riders in their fabled charge up San Juan Hill during the Spanish-American War of 1898. Roosevelt's heroism in Cuba helped elevate him to national prominence, and within three years he was president.

Harvard University. It had been Theodore's intention to become a zoologist, but when his father died suddenly in 1878 he decided to stay close to home. In 1880 he married Alice Hathaway Lee, whom he'd met while attending Harvard. He enrolled in Columbia University in New York with the intention of studying law, but he soon grew bored with his classes. He became a writer, authoring books on history and the outdoors. Finally, in 1882, Theodore learned that the local Republican club was looking for a candidate for the New York State Assembly, the governing body that writes laws for the state government. He decided to pursue a career in politics.

He impressed Republican leaders, who supported him for the office. Theodore won the election.

For the next 16 years Theodore Roosevelt would climb steadily up the political ladder. But in his personal life he experienced tragedy. In 1884, Alice Roosevelt died while giving birth to the couple's daughter. "When my heart's dearest died, the light went from my life forever," Roosevelt wrote. After enduring a bout of depression following the death of his wife, Roosevelt began seeing Edith Carow, a friend since childhood. They married in 1886.

In 1895 Roosevelt took on the job of police commissioner of New York City, and in 1897 he accepted a job in Washington as assistant secretary of the navy. When the Spanish-American War broke out in 1898, Roosevelt left Washington to join the Rough Riders. Following the Battle of San Juan Hill he became such a celebrity that, upon returning home, he had no difficulty winning election as governor of New York. In 1900, William McKinley asked him to join the ticket as his candidate for vice president. After just six months as president, McKinley died from the gunshot wound inflicted by Czolgosz, and Theodore Roosevelt became the 26th president of the United States.

As president, Teddy Roosevelt quickly made his mark on American history. One of his first acts was to bring a lawsuit against a railroad that had grown into a *monopoly*, also known as a "trust." Roosevelt believed that when a company grew too big and dominated its business, competitors and customers suffered because the big company could control prices. The courts ruled in favor of the president. He became known as the

Although presidents as far back as John Adams lived in the Executive Mansion in Washington, Theodore Roosevelt was the first president to add the address "White House" to his official stationery.

"trustbuster" for his efforts to break up monopolies.

In the early years of the 20th century most Americans heated their homes with coal. In May 1902, coal miners went on strike seeking higher wages. In the past, most presidents had stayed out of labor issues, believing companies had a right to work out their own problems. But in this case, the strike threatened the ability of Americans to stay warm in the winter. Teddy Roosevelt sent federal troops onto the mine properties to safeguard the mines from vandals and protect striking workers from *thugs* hired by the coal companies. Next, he brought leaders of the coal companies and strikers to Washington and helped them reach a settlement.

Roosevelt was fond of the expression "Speak softly and carry a big stick." By that, he meant that it was always best to talk over problems, but if talking failed, a president should never hesitate to use the might of the American military. In foreign affairs, Teddy was not afraid to commit troops to a region where he believed other countries threatened America's international interests. In Central America, he supported Panamanian rebels fighting for independence from Colombia. After the Panamanians won their independence, the American government bought a 50-mile strip of land across the *isthmus* of Panama. There the United States began construction of the Panama Canal.

After serving out McKinley's term, Roosevelt was elected

A ship plies the Panama Canal, the construction of which is considered one of Theodore Roosevelt's many important achievements as president.

to a full term of his own in 1904. He chose not to run in 1908, but soon found himself fighting with Republican leaders about the direction of the party.

In 1912, Teddy ran for the Republican nomination again. He failed to win the support of political leaders, so he quickly formed his own party, the Progressive Party. When he was wounded that year in an assassination attempt, he joked, "It takes more than that to kill a bull moose." Soon, his party came to be known as the Bull Moose Party. His campaign for president failed, though, and Roosevelt retired from politics.

In 1914, still an avid outdoorsman, he explored jungles in South America. During the grueling expedition he became quite sick, but eventually he recovered.

He died on January 6, 1919, in Oyster Bay, New York.

CHRONOLOGY

1858 Theodore Roosevelt is born in New York City.

1872 After being bullied on a stagecoach trip to Maine, Theodore Roosevelt decides to devote himself to physical fitness; Roosevelt family begins overseas trip that will take them to North Africa, the Middle East, and Europe.

1873 Theodore Roosevelt studies in Dresden, Germany.

1880 Graduates from Harvard University.

1895 Named police commissioner of New York City.

1897 Appointed assistant secretary of the U.S. Navy.

1898 Resigns from navy to join the Rough Riders, a volunteer cavalry unit fighting in the Spanish-American War; elected governor of New York State.

1901 Takes office as vice president of the United States; becomes president following the assassination of President McKinley.

1903 Construction of the Panama Canal begins; Roosevelt spearheads effort to preserve 230 million acres of American land by developing a system of national parks and forests.

1904 Elected to a full term as president.

1905 Wins Nobel Peace Prize for brokering a peace in the Russo-Japanese War.

1909 Presidency ends.

1912 Runs unsuccessfully for president as a member of the Progressive Party.

1919 Dies in Oyster Bay, New York.

ancestor—someone from whom a person or a group of people are descended.

bookish—having a love for reading and learning.

conservationist—a person who works to preserve nature.

devious—given to clever and often dishonest plotting.

dissect—to cut open the body of a dead animal for the purposes of study.

Frau—in the German language, a married woman; as a title, Frau means "Mrs."

girth—the measure of an object or a body around the midsection.

isthmus—a narrow strip of land connecting two larger landmasses and bordered on both sides by water.

jackal—a type of wild dog, found mostly in Africa and Asia.

monopoly—a company that controls the marketplace for a particular type of product or service.

mosque—a building used for worship in the religion of Islam.

nearsighted—unable to see objects at a distance clearly.

prizefighter—an athlete who boxes for cash rewards.

sickly—having a tendency to be ill frequently.

thug—a person who makes a living hurting or killing people for hire.

zoologist—a scientist who studies animals.

FURTHER READING

Churchill, Allen. *The Roosevelts: American Aristocrats*. New York: Harper and Row, 1965.

Kozar, Richard. *Theodore Roosevelt and the Exploration of the Amazon Basin*. Philadelphia: Chelsea House, 2001.

Marten, James. *The Children's Civil War*. Chapel Hill: University of North Carolina Press, 1998.

McCullough, David. *Mornings on Horseback*. New York: Simon and Schuster, 1981.

Morris, Edmund. *The Rise of Theodore Roosevelt*. New York: Coward, McCann and Geoghegan, 1979.

Roosevelt, Theodore. *An Autobiography*. New York: Da Capo Press, 1985.

Rubel, David. *The Scholastic Encyclopedia of the Presidents and Their Times*. New York: Agincourt Press, 1994.

Schuman, Michael A. *Theodore Roosevelt*. Springfield, N.J.: Enslow Publishers, 1997.

- http://www.pbs.org/wgbh/amex/presidents/nf/featured/tr/trec.html
  The American Experience: Theodore Roosevelt

- http://memory.loc.gov/ammem/trfhtml/trfhome.html
  Theodore Roosevelt: His Life and Times on Film

- http://www.theodoreroosevelt.org/
  The Theodore Roosevelt Association

- http://theodore-roosevelt-national-historic-site.visit-new-york-city.com/
  Theodore Roosevelt National Historic Site

- http://www.theodore-roosevelt.com
  Theodore Roosevelt: 26th President of the United States of America

- http://www.whitehouse.gov/history/presidents/tr26.html
  The White House Biography of Theodore Roosevelt

INDEX

Contributors

ARTHUR M. SCHLESINGER JR. holds the Albert Schweitzer Chair in the Humanities at the Graduate Center of the City University of New York. He is the author of more than a dozen books, including *The Age of Jackson*; *The Vital Center*; *The Age of Roosevelt* (3 vols.); *A Thousand Days: John F. Kennedy in the White House*; *Robert Kennedy and His Times*; *The Cycles of American History*; and *The Imperial Presidency*. Professor Schlesinger served as Special Assistant to President Kennedy (1961–63). His numerous awards include the Pulitzer Prize for History; the Pulitzer Prize for Biography; two National Book Awards; the Bancroft Prize; and the American Academy of Arts and Letters Gold Medal for History.

HAL MARCOVITZ is a journalist for *The Morning Call*, a newspaper based in Allentown, Pennsylvania. He has written more than 30 books for young readers. He lives in Chalfont, Pennsylvania, with his wife, Gail, and daughters Ashley and Michelle.